SOUTH ARRAN – A Postcard

by Ken Hall

First Published in the United Kingdom, 1994
By Richard Stenlake, Ochiltree Sawmill, The Lade, Ochiltree, Ayrshire _____ ___
Telephone: 0290 700266   01290 700266 (from April 1995)

ISBN 1-872074-36-7

FOREWORD

Following on from the North Arran Tour, this book begins at the String Road which traverses the centre of the island.

The scenes round the south end of the island may lack the grandeur of the hills, but this is more than made up for by the Clyde and Argyll views, the agriculture and the busy resorts of Whiting Bay and Lamlash.

Many of these postcards reflect dramatic changes in agricultural methods and in modes of transport on both land and sea, to which the unchanging coastal scenery provides a perfect foil.

The 'String' road rises from Brodick on the east coast, to a height of 234m, before descending into Shiskine and eventually Blackwaterfoot on the west coast.

Colin Currie, postman, is seen here approaching the summit, with Glensherraig and Brodick Bay in the background.

1

At this intersection, known as the Machrie Road End, there stands a unique pillar box.

In the 1880s, when the original white pillar box caused a horse to shie in fright throwing the young girl rider to the ground, the Duke of Hamilton commissioned a box to be built that blended in better with the rustic landscape. The large sum provided, fifty pounds, meant that the job was done in grand style – the stone mason, David Wilson, spun the work out by decorating the Arran stone structure with Mason's marks.

In the 1960s, when the level of the road surface was raised, the apparent height of the pillar box was greatly reduced and in June 1993 it was accidentally demolished by a car. However a local builder, Ian Stewart of Shiskine, recovered the original stones and with the help of postcards, including this 1911 view, drawings and photographs, had rebuilt the box by November that same year. The bonus is that it is now standing at its original height in relation to the road surface.

The area known as Shiskine was a convenient halfway house for postal services from Brodick to the Machrie as well as to the Blackwaterfoot areas.

The two horse brake was operated by Colin Currie, a man of large stature, who became a postman at the age of 17, in 1866, and gave 47 years service as postman in Shiskine (note the long service bars on his chest). He also farmed at Balmichael Farm and in 1913 introduced the island's first omnibus – an Albion. This scene shows the arrival of the brake at Shedog in 1908.

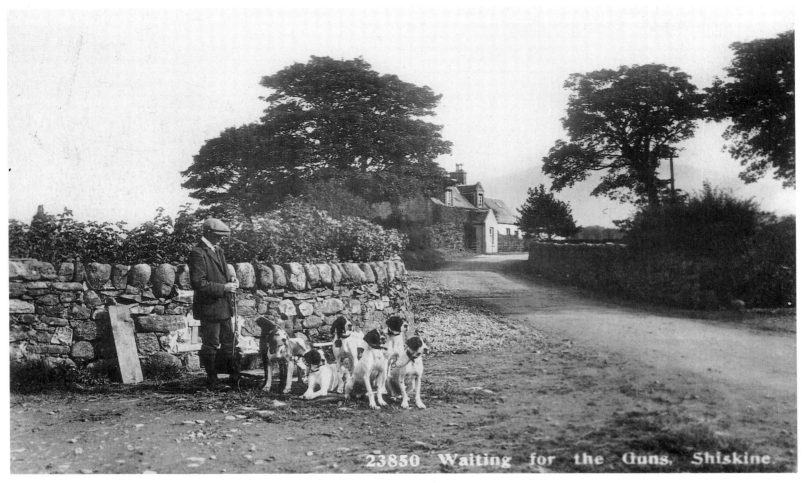

23850 Waiting for the Guns, Shiskine.

This part of Shiskine is known locally as Shedog, which comes from the Gaelic Sheidog meaning windy place. In this 1916 view, the dogs are standing across the road from the Hamilton Arms Hotel.

HAMILTON ARMS HOTEL, SHISKINE, ARRAN

These details are from an invoice dated 1876:

Proprietor: George Wooley

2 Breakfasts	4/-
Beds	3/6d
Attendance	1.6d
Stabling	3/-
	Settled 12/-

Hamilton Arms Inn
Shiskine
Arran

The building now provides accommodation for The Arran Outdoor Centre.

Cottages at Skiskine. The thatch on these 1903 cottages is not in good repair but the peat stack is well built and tidy. The peats themselves would probably have come from the Machrie Moor, where they would have been cut, dried and stored over the summer months.

The first aeroplane to land on Arran did so in the Corrygills district near Brodick sometime around 1929.

In the 1930s a small airstrip was in use at Shiskine. The houses of Shedog can be seen behind this "Midlands & Scottish Air Ferries Ltd. plane. If requested, the Glasgow-Campbeltown regular service would land to pick up or disembark passengers. In 1935, a 4-seater plane gave pleasure flights round the valley for 5 shillings and for 25 shillings, you could get a flight round the island.

The location is unclear, but this photograph of Colin Currie's horse brakes was probably taken on or near his home farm of Balmichael, just north of Shiskine. This looks like some special event, as everyone seems to be very well dressed!

WASHING DAY, SHISKINE, ARRAN.

Just imagine: the fire to be kindled, the huge boiler to be heated, then hot water into the wash tub and all that energy used on the scrubbing board, not to mention the rinsing and hanging out to dry!

23837 Harvest Scene, Shiskine.

A field of oats being cut by a three-horse binder, probably on the Balnacoole farmland, just south of Balmichael farm, near Shedog. The cut and bound sheaves have already been put into "stooks" of six sheaves each and will ripen and dry out for at least two weeks before being carted off and stacked into corn stacks. Later in the winter the sheaves of corn will be threshed and the oats used as animal feed. Some will be kept for seed the next year. The straw will be used for fodder and bedding.

SHISKINE VALLEY, BLACKWATERFOOT.

Torbeg Farm, with the peaks of Ben Nuis and Goatfell to the north. The stallion is being walked on his round to put mares into foal.

Hay-making at Torbeg Farm.

The process started by cutting mature grass with a two-horse reaper, leaving it out to dry in the swathe for a day or two, then turning the swathe for further drying. When judged to be sufficiently dry, the swathes of hay were collected by a hay rake into lines across the field. Next, a five-pronged hay collector, pulled by a horse and called a "tumbling tam", collected the hay around a chosen spot where the hay rick was to be built. The hay was then built into the rick using pitch forks.

These ricks allowed the hay to further mature and dry out, till they were finally carted off the field and built into stacks. Thus fodder was preserved for the winter months.

Hay-making was heavy work as it always took place in dry, hot, sunny weather.

Unloading at Blackwaterfoot.

The puffer has managed to get up the burn and carts can be manoeuvred alongside, to be loaded with coal.

14

Fishing boats in Blackwaterfoot. This scene, prior to 1886, shows the old wooden bridge before the present stone bridge was built. A ford upstream of the wooden bridge took the heavier horse-drawn traffic.

Blackwaterfoot from the Port

JV 79545

This 1914 photograph, shows Colin Currie's first bus, an Albion purchased in 1913, about to cross the stone bridge. The small shed to the right of the bus is the public "weigh house". To the left is the store, built in 1886 and further to the left is the ferryman's cottage. The white buildings above are the stables.

TEMPERANCE HOTEL, BLACKWATERFOOT.

This building was empty and facing an uncertain future, but has recently opened as a hotel which serves wine and spirits – gone are the days when Blackwaterfoot was considered a "dry" area!

The horse and trap was a relatively swift and comfortable mode of transport, if the weather was dry!

INTRUSIVE SILL, DRUMADOON, ISLAND OF ARRAN.

A sill of igneous rock (quartz-porphyry) which, while molten lava, was squeezed into sedimentary rocks to form a sheet parallel to the strata. The underlying sediments (Triassic sandstones and shales) are seen towards the left. Notice the columnar character of the jointing of the sill.

Known as the "Doon", this volcanic rock is a very dominant landmark on the coast, at the head of Drumadoon Bay. On top are the remains of an old fort. The path to the Kings Caves passes beneath the columnar structure. The caves providing a hiding place at one time for Robert Bruce.

Blackwaterfoot Golf Club House in 1908.

This course is almost unique, in that it is a 12-hole course. The original 9-hole course was extended to an 18 hole course in 1913 when an extra 6 holes were laid out on the hill directly behind the clubhouse.

Club House and Home Green, Golf Course, Blackwaterfoot, Arran

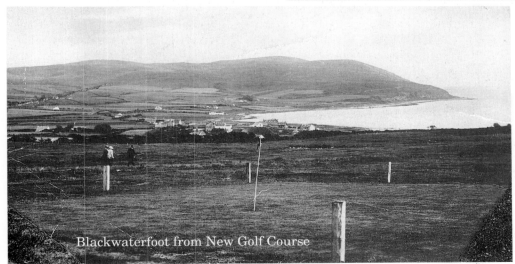

Blackwaterfoot from New Golf Course

The full course was in use for about 10 years but fell into disuse as the effort to climb up to the 6 extra holes dissuaded many golfers from using them and only 12 holes were subsequently used.

19

The Sands, Blackwaterfoot

The beach within Drumadoon Bay is sandy and shelves very slowly into deeper water, making it a relatively safe beach for bathers. Drumadoon Point and the Kintyre Peninsula can be seen in the background. Parties of residents from the Hamilton Arms at Shedog would often be bussed down to the beach to spend a day on the sands and enjoy the shore. This 1913 scene could have been just such an occasion.

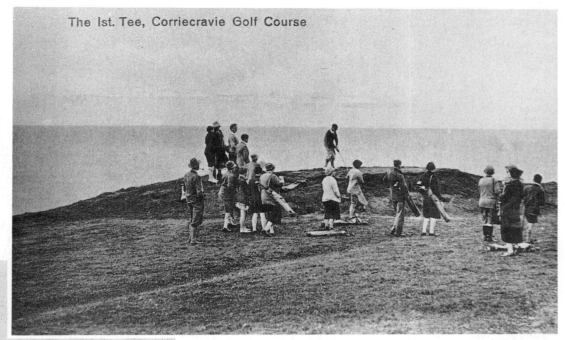

The Ist. Tee, Corriecravie Golf Course

South of Blackwaterfoot, on the coast road, the area known as Corriecravie clings to the steep-sided coastline, with views across the Kilbrannan Sound to Campbeltown Loch. The road then winds on to Sliddery.

This 9-hole golf course was opened around 1911 and was in use until it was ploughed up during the 1939-45 war.

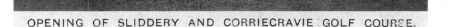

OPENING OF SLIDDERY AND CORRIECRAVIE GOLF COURSE.

Sliddery, like Corriecravie, is more an area rather than a village as such. Within the area there were to be found a shoemaker, blacksmith, butcher and joiner's business. This building, built in 1860, housed the school until 1948, when pupils were transferred to Kilmorie. It then became a post office and grocery business, which closed down on 31 October 1981.

22

The ground at Whitefield Farm has been ploughed by the pair of horses. Corn is being sown by hand and the seed covered by the set of horse-drawn harrows. Note the lady carrying more corn in her bucket to replenish the sower, so that he does not lose his marks.

D. McNeish & Sons store at Sliddery, in 1909, with the origins of the mobile shop, advertising their trade as bakers, grocers and general merchants.

The Smithy, Sliddery.

The original sub post office opened in 1898 beside the village smithy and was run by a Miss Ferguson. Later the sub post office was transferred to the village school master, Robert Cook, who used the porch of the school house as a post office.

On Clachaig Farm, Kilmorie.

A typical herd of Ayrshire cows, with horns. Since the 1950s, the horned cow breeds of cattle are dehorned routinely soon after the calves are born. The "horn buds" are treated to prevent any growth. At one time on Clachaig Farm there was a tile-works for making draining tiles, the clay being dug from the lower end of some of the fields. Some of the land in this area is of the "heavy" clay type of soil, as distinct from the more normal sandy loams.

26

An end of harvest scene in the stackyard of Clachaig Farm.

Note how some of the stacks of corn sheaves have already been thatched, probably with rushes, and roped down to keep the corn dry till the sheaves are threshed.

The hotel at Lagg, parts of which date back to 1791, has a very striking appearance. It is situated in a hollow beside the river and palm trees flourish within its grounds. This photograph shows the hotel in 1925.

There is known to have been a distillery at Lagg around 1800 and the kiln, where the grain was crushed and dried, can still be identified at Clachaig.

The arrival of the daily bus service was no doubt quite an event!

Shannochie Post Office.   Isle of Arran.

Shannochie sub post office, seen here circa 1904/5, was opened in 1898. In later years it moved to the thatched cottage of Mrs Hamilton. When she died the office was taken over by her daughter, Miss Jenny Hamilton, until she died in 1977. At that time it was one of the last post offices in Scotland to have a thatched roof.

prescription bottles left with her

29

COTTAGES - LENAMHOR, S. ARRAN.

These cottages, pictured here in 1909, are situated in the area known as West Bennan, on the south coast of Arran, above Bennan Head.

BREADALBANE BOARDING HOUSE, KILDONAN ARRAN.   210898 J.V.

Kildonan has always been a popular place for holiday-makers. This hotel looks out over the natural harbour to Pladda island. In summer many seals can be seen basking on the rocks of the bay, just offshore.

This was always a busy corner of the village. Up until 1946, smacks and puffers came into the port with coal, building materials and provisions from the mainland. Close beside the port were housed a shoemaker, tailor, smithy, local shop, meal mill, church and school.

Kildonan Hotel, pictured here in 1908 is reputed to be one of the oldest hotels on the island and was in existence in 1800. The Jamieson brothers, who ran the hotel in the early 1900s, provided this conveyance to and from the pier at Whiting Bay. In 1914, it was replaced by a motor omnibus.

Auchenhew Bay, Kildonan.

77617. J.V.

The view is typical of the coastline around South Arran where the shores are dominated by cliffs and raised beaches, the rocky coastline the cause of many shipwrecks. Kildonan was the site of the island's only Coastguard Station which closed in 1981.

Cottages at Kildonan

21·7·03.

Craigus

Very wet
today,
but am
enjoying
myself
very
much
indeed.

These
are
the kind
of cottages
to be

found in Arran.

The village of Kildonan originated from small clachans, dotted round the district. The majority of villagers were engaged in farming and a lot of this was carried out in the run-rig system.

Kildonan Castle is supposed to have been one of the line of forts built by Alexander II and it remained a Royal Castle till 1405. Latterly it was used as a hunting seat by Scottish Kings.

The Ross Road is the other road to traverse the island. It runs from just north of Kilmory across to Lamlash. This location on the road was known as the Iron Bridge.

A Cave Dwelling, West Coast of Arran.

E 18157

Caves are numerous around the South Arran coastline and many were put to use as dwellings. The largest cave on the island, called the Monster or Black Cave, is to be found at Bennan Head, where the cliffs are up to 457 feet high. As with the cave at Kilpatrick, it was once used as a place of worship by the islanders and relics of habitation – arrowheads, flints, shells etc., have been found inside. The last occupants of the cave were probably travelling people, who found temporary work in the summer months and sold small items door-to-door around the island.

Portleck

3.7.06

Isn't this a lovely view? It is just a short distance from us.

This shows pockets of good land down on shore level, with the usual backdrop of cliffs. The buildings form a clachan between Kildonan and Dippen Head.

Dippen Head is a promontory at the south eastern extremity of Arran, east of the Kildonan district. The precipices rise sheer to 300 feet above the shore line.

Seacliffe, Dippen.

The long black houses of clachans were built of double courses of dry stone, rubble cored and plastered on the inside with clay. They were thatched with heather, or less frequently straw, laid over turfs resting on brushwood.

Waiting for the steamer, Whiting Bay. A regular sailing service from Saltcoats to Whiting Bay was started about 1770, a steamer service from Glasgow began in about 1829 and, when the railway to Ardrossan had been completed, there was a steamer service from there. There were no piers, in those days, so passengers were landed by ferry boat at Kings Cross, or onto the stone jetty at Whiting Bay.

This pier, the last to be built, was opened in 1899 and was the longest pier in the Firth of Clyde. It continued in use till 1962 and was finally dismantled in 1964. This 1905 postcard shows wagonettes at the pierhead waiting to take passengers to their final destination. Jamiesons wagonette is on the right of the picture.

By the early 1930s, motorised transport had all but taken over from the horse-drawn vehicles.

This pier was the last port of call on the run from Ardrossan via Brodick, Lamlash and Kings Cross, before returning by the same route. Steamers spent almost as much time distributing passengers along the shores, between Brodick and Whiting Bay, as they took to do the actual crossing of the Firth.

Whiting Bay has always been a popular holiday resort. Golf, bowling and tennis in the village, plus many fine walks, especially up Glen Ashdale to the Falls or along the shore, meant many holiday pursuits were within easy reach.

Harvesting, Sand Braes, Whiting Bay.

1923. A fine pair of white horses is pulling the reaper as the extra man on the "tilting board" makes the bunches. Three men behind are making sheaves from the bunches, then stooking them. It looks as though the lassie on the right has brought the "tea basket" and is waiting to catch the horseman's eye!

This field was a putting green owned by a Captain Mathie 1p per ound (18 holes). Where I polished my golf!

44

The gentler slopes above Whiting Bay are agricultural. Kings Cross Point and Holy Isle can be seen north of the bay.

Kerr's Stores, Whiting Bay

A typical village store of the period; selling shoes, stationery, sweets and tobacco. Postcard views hang in the window and a penny weighing machine is placed strategically at the side of the shop! The building is still in use today – electricians on the left and post office on the right.

The Polytechnic, Auchencairn, Whiting Bay.

This particular shop was established before the First World War, in 1912, and the premises were in use until the business moved to Sandbraes, in Whiting Bay itself, around 1916. Alexander McKelvie also operated a van which served the south end of the island and Lamlash. Like many other stores, they also published local postcard views.

Giants' Graves, Largiemore. Isle of Arran.

Published by Finlay Boa, Kildonan, P. O.

On the hill above Glen Ashdale, overlooking Whiting Bay, are the burial cairn and standing stones known as the "Giant's Graves". Two standing stones mark the semi-circle of the cairn, within which there are three chambered tombs. Some fragments found were identified as burnt human bones – evidence of cremation. Today the site is within the forest.

48

J. Cooks store and post office, in 1925, with the Lamlash to Kings Cross bus. The post office was established in 1880 and was run by only two sub-postmasters over the space of almost a century – the Cooks – father and son. When Alan Cook died, in 1978, the post office closed. The post box – set in the wall of the house – was unique in that it had a brass flap marked "letters".

Where we did our shopping when we had a house round the corner

E 18186

The Ferry, King's Cross, Isle of Arran

The landing stage where steamer passengers were landed or picked up by the ferry boat. Across the water can be seen Holy Island and the lighthouse station.

Used to play, sometimes swim here

Passengers landing at King's Cross Ferry.

The delicate operation of transferring passengers from the steamer onto the ferry boat.

Robert the Bruce's Cairn, King's Cross. Isle of Arran. E 18219

Robert the Bruce spent some time in Arran before crossing to Ayrshire. A fire at Turnberry Point was to be the signal to Bruce that all was well and that the coast was clear.

According to one version of the story, the observed blaze was not the awaited signal and was probably caused by a farmer burning straw. Bruce and his followers set sail from King's Cross Point and arrived at Turnberry to find everything in chaos! It was too late to retreat but despite this setback, Bruce went on to victory.

A regular picnic/swimming spot

Isle of Arran   *Hamilton Terrace, Lamlash*

The houses of Hamilton Terrace are made of stone from a harbour which was originally built by The Duchess Anne of Hamilton.

Built around 1895, it is thought to have been the first street in the village.

The post office is still in the same building today.

Lamlash Pier and Bowling Green   J. of Arran

This pier was built, in 1887, to replace the old one. It in turn was demolished between 1950 and 1954.

The bay, with its protection of the Holy Isle, is a very safe anchorage and was used as a naval base, particularly during the two World Wars. Because naval personnel were given courtesy of the golf course, the Navy presented trophies to the golf club which are still played for today.

There is a lot of very fertile soil around this district and some of the largest and most productive farms on the island are in the area.

Donald McKelvie O.B.E., who grew and bred seed potatoes, produced over 30 new varieties, all with the ARRAN prefix, between 1908 and 1947. The gold medals, which he received for his achievements, can be seen in the Arran Heritage Museum.

Old Nicol Street, Lamlash

545/210

The site is now the end of Park Terrace. It is known that amongst those people who lived here, occupations ranged from dressmaker, pier hand, thatcher/dry stane dyker, fruiterer, builder, gardener, estate worker, coastguard, general worker, roadman, and van driver!